BRIGHT
IDEA
BOOKS

AMAZING HUMAN FEATS OF Engineering

by Matt Scheff

raintree

a Capstone company — publishers for children

Raintree is an imprint of Capstone Global Library Limited, a company incorporated in England and Wales having its registered office at 264 Banbury Road, Oxford, OX2 7DY – Registered company number: 6695582

www.raintree.co.uk
myorders@raintree.co.uk

Edited by Meg Gaertner
Designed by Becky Daum
Production by Craig Hinton
Originated by Capstone Global Library Ltd
Printed and bound in India

ISBN 978 1 4747 7522 9   ISBN 978 1 4747 7346 1
22 21 20 19 18   23 22 21 20 19
10 9 8 7 6 5 4 3 2 1   10 9 8 7 6 5 4 3 2 1

British Library Cataloguing in Publication Data
A full catalogue record for this book is available from the British Library.

Acknowledgements
We would like to thank the following for permission to reproduce photographs: AP Images: Ross D. Franklin, 22–23; iStockphoto: garyperkin, 18–19, georgeclerk, 17, Marc-Andre_LeTourneux, 12–13, powerofforever, 11, vgajic, 31; NASA: JSC/NASA, 15; Shutterstock Images: Anton Gvozdikov, 8–9, aphotostory, 5, Naufal MQ, 8, nootprapa, 21, Pius Lee, 25, 28, Prin Adulyatham, 26–27, S-F, 7, shutterlk, cover. Design Elements: iStockphoto, Red Line Editorial, and Shutterstock Images.

Every effort has been made to contact copyright holders of material reproduced in this book. Any omissions will be rectified in subsequent printings if notice is given to the publisher.

All the internet addresses (URLs) given in this book were valid at the time of going to press. However, due to the dynamic nature of the internet, some addresses may have changed, or sites may have changed or ceased to exist since publication. While the author and publisher regret any inconvenience this may cause readers, no responsibility for any such changes can be accepted by either the author or the publisher.

CONTENTS

CHAPTER ONE
ENGINEERING

CHAPTER TWO
TOUCHING THE SKY

CHAPTER THREE
THE POWER OF WATER

CHAPTER FOUR
OUT OF THIS WORLD

CHAPTER FIVE
UNDER THE SEA

CHAPTER SIX
AN AMAZING VIEW

CHAPTER SEVEN
ANCIENT GIANT

Glossary 28
Other amazing feats............. 29
Activity 30
Find out more 32
Index..................................... 32

CHAPTER 1

ENGINEERING

A tower rises above the clouds. A train runs under the sea. A space station **orbits** Earth. A **pyramid** stands for almost 5,000 years.

These are all feats of engineering. People have been building since ancient times. They make careful plans. They achieve amazing feats.

The Great Wall of China was built over a period of 2,000 years.

CHAPTER 2

TOUCHING THE
Sky

The Burj Khalifa is the world's tallest tower. It is in Dubai in the United Arab Emirates. The tower is 828 metres (2,717 feet) tall. It has more than 160 floors.

TALL TOWERS

The Shanghai Tower in China is almost as tall. It is 632 metres (2,073 feet) tall.

The Three Gorges Dam was finished in 2006. It spans a river in China. It is the world's biggest **concrete** structure. It is 185 metres (607 feet) tall. It is 2,335 metres (7,660 feet) long.

The Three Gorges Dam is the world's largest hydroelectric dam.

CHAPTER 4

OUT OF THIS
World

The International Space Station (ISS) was built in space. It is more than 400 kilometres (248 miles) above Earth. It is the largest man-made object in space. It is as long as a football pitch.

ISS VIEWING

People on Earth can see the ISS with a small telescope.

Hundreds of people have visited the station. The ISS is home to about six people at a time.

Astronauts go on spacewalks to fix or add to the ISS.

CHAPTER 5

UNDER THE Sea

The **Channel** Tunnel connects England and France. It is the world's longest underwater tunnel. More than 37 kilometres (23 miles) of the tunnel are under the sea.

Visitors can board a train in London that takes them all the way to Paris.

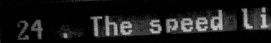

UNDERWATER TRIP

The Channel Tunnel is around 50 metres (165 feet) below the sea floor. A railway runs inside the tunnel. Trains carry people, goods and cars. More than 10 million people use the tunnel each year. A trip takes only about 20 minutes.

CONSTRUCTION

It took 13,000 workers six years to build the Channel Tunnel.

Cars drive into the train. The train will carry them through the tunnel.

TOUGH AS GLASS

The Skywalk is 21 metres (70 feet) long. It is very heavy and strong.

Only 120 people can be on the Skywalk at once. But it can support more than 800. It was built to stand up to earthquakes.

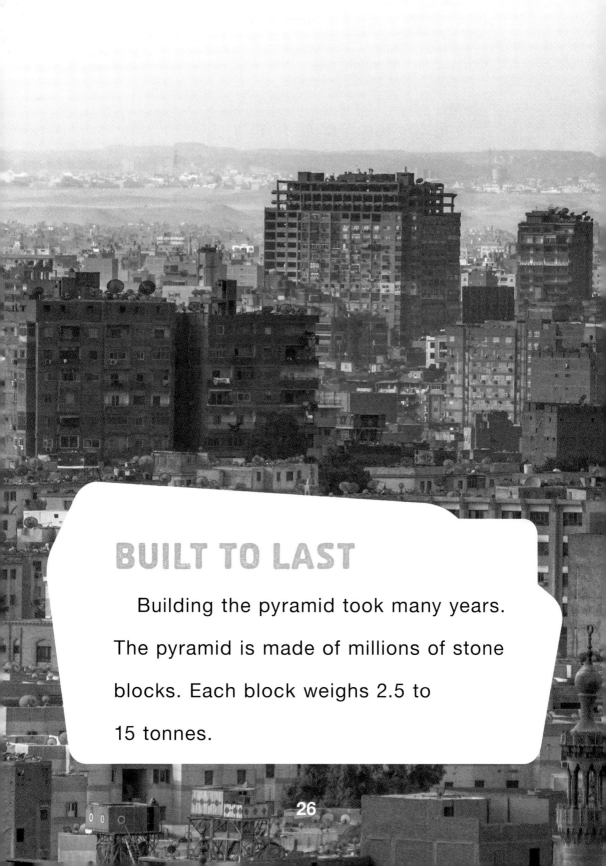

BUILT TO LAST

Building the pyramid took many years. The pyramid is made of millions of stone blocks. Each block weighs 2.5 to 15 tonnes.

CHAPTER 7

ANCIENT
Giant

Some building feats come from long ago. The Great Pyramid at Giza in Egypt was built almost 5,000 years ago.

DRY DESERT

Egypt's dry air keeps the Great Pyramid in good condition.

Tourists take photos
of the view.

31

FIND OUT MORE

Are you amazed by these feats of engineering and curious to learn more? Check out these resources:

Books

Engineering Projects to Build On (STEM Projects), Tammy Enz (Raintree, 2019)

Extraordinary Skyscrapers (Exceptional Engineering), Sonya Newland (Raintree, 2019)

Great British Engineering (Best of British), Claire Throp (Raintree, 2018)

The World's Most Amazing Stadiums (Landmark Top Tens), Michael Hurley (Raintree, 2012)

Websites

Watch the clips to learn more about how the pyramids were built.
www.bbc.com/bitesize/clips/z849wmn

Find out more about landmarks of the world.
www.dkfindout.com/uk/earth/landmarks-world

INDEX

Burj Khalifa 6–9

Channel Tunnel 16–18

dams 10–12

Grand Canyon 20
Great Pyramid 24–27

International Space Station (ISS) 14–15

pyramids 4, 24–27

Skywalk 20–22
space station 4, 14–15

Three Gorges Dam 11–12
towers 4, 6–9
trains 4, 18

viewing decks 9, 20–22